Picnic Party

Ryan the Lion and the Otter Twins are ready for some fresh air, good food, and fun and games. And they want *you* to join them! Let's all go to the picnic, and play some cool games using multiplication and division.

You will have fun with the following activities:

- Relating Addition to Multiplication
- Identifying and Estimating
- Multiplication and Division

See you in the park!

Logic Feature

Each person brought a different item to the picnic.

Ina did **not** bring the hot dogs or the cookies.

Al did **not** bring the cookies or the drinks.

Ken did **not** bring the hot dogs or the drinks.

Brenda always brings the salad.

Use the clues above to mark the chart and figure out who brought what.

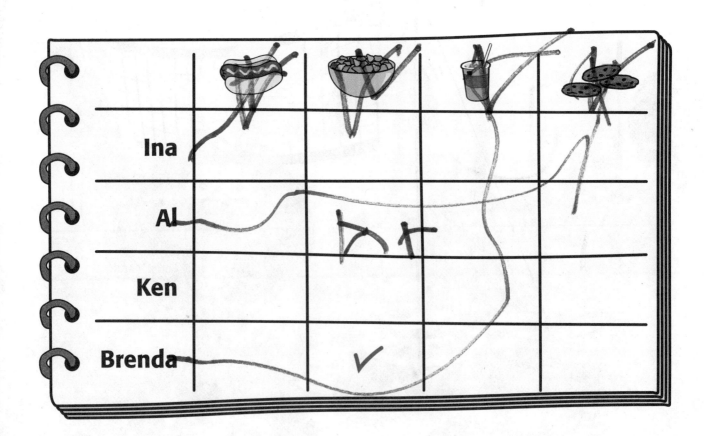

Start with any of the numbers in the top row. Multiply it by 2. Move to the seed in the second row that has your answer. Multiply that number by 3. Now move to the seed in the next row that has your answer on it. Continue this way, multiplying by 4, 5, and 6 until you get to the bottom row. **Hint:** As you go, trace your way by putting your finger on the numbers.

> We did an example for you! See? $3 \times 2 = 6$, $3 \times 3 = 9$, $3 \times 4 = 12$. Try it with the other numbers!

1	2	3	4	5	6	7	8	9	10
10	8	18	6	14	4	2	12	20	16
12	3	18	15	24	21	30	27	9	6
36	28	24	40	20	4	8	12	32	16
5	20	35	50	10	15	40	30	50	45	25
54	30	12	24	48	60	6	18	36	42

Adding Repeated Numbers

Draw a line from the repeated addition problem to the multiplication equation it represents.

When you add one number to the same number and then again to the same number, that's called repeated addition.

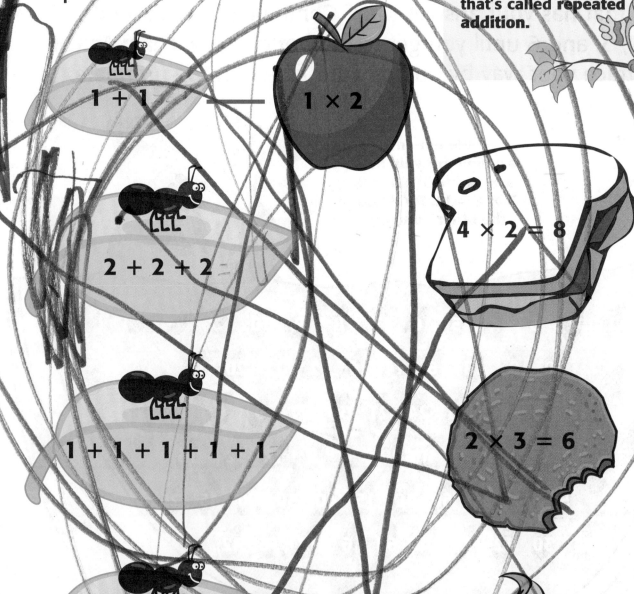

$1 + 1$

1×2

$2 + 2 + 2$

$4 \times 2 = 8$

$1 + 1 + 1 + 1 + 1$

$2 \times 3 = 6$

$4 + 4$

$1 \times 5 = 5$

Use repeated addition to create multiplication equations.

Steven loved to help his mother plan the family picnic. "We will make hot dogs," said his mother. "Let's see—there will be you, me, Dad, and your sister. That makes four people." "Each person eats two hot dogs. So 2 + 2 + 2 + 2 = 8," said Steven. "There is a shortcut you could use," said his mother, "2 _____ + _____ = 8." "Let's also make s'mores. I love s'mores," said Steven. "We could each eat six of those," said his mother. "OK, then 6 + 6 + 6 + 6 = 24," said Steven. "Now wait," said his mother, "You can multiply. _____ + _____ + 4 = 24." "Thanks for helping me multiply," Steven told his mother. "This picnic will be lots of fun!"

Solve problems 1 through 5 below by multiplying the food items by the number listed in each equation. Draw a picture to help you solve each problem.

1. $7 \times$ 🌭 $= 14$

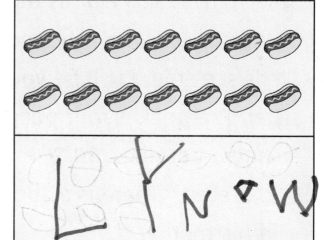

2. $5 \times$ 🍔 $= 1$

3. 🍉 $\times 2 = 2$

4. $6 \times$ 🥪 $= 12$

5. 🍦 $\times 2 = 1$

The Otter Twins have found out that there will be four times as many people at their picnic than they had expected. Use the numbers on their original shopping list to help them make a new shopping list for the picnic.

You can help by multiplying each number by 4.

Grocery List

hot dogs—4 packages

hamburgers—8 packages

chips—5 bags

cookies—3 dozen

fruit drink—7 bottles

Grocery List

4 × 4 = 16 hot dogs

Ryan the Lion needs $22. He has saved $6. His grandmother gave him $10 more. He has to do odd jobs to earn the rest. Each job pays $2. How many jobs will Ryan need to do?

Work backward to find your answer!

Step 1: The money Ryan wants to have − the money he has saved = the money he still needs

_____22_____ − _____6_____ = _____

Step 2: The money Ryan needs (the answer from Step 1) − the money his grandmother gave him = the money Ryan must earn

_____ − _____ = _____

Step 3: The money Ryan must earn (the answer from Step 2) ÷ the amount of money for each job = the number of odd jobs Ryan needs to do

_____ ÷ _____ = _____

Ryan needs to do _____ jobs.

Use the words in the word box to help you complete the crossword puzzle.

four	sixteen	thirty	twenty
eighteen	ten	twelve	nine
eight	six	fifteen	

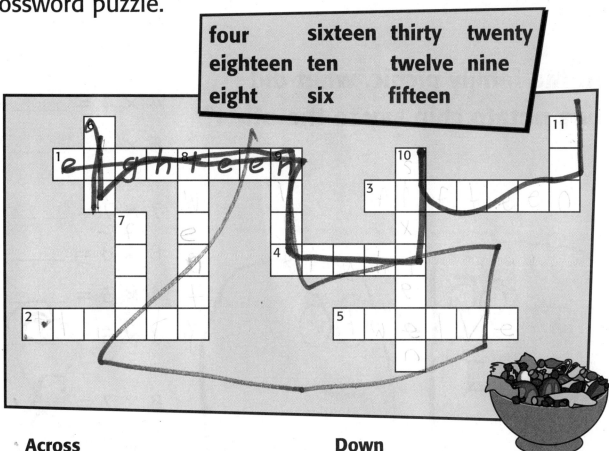

Across

1. Joey's mom brought three 6-packs of fruit drink for the picnic. How many cans of fruit drink did she buy?

2. 5 × 6

3. 3 × 5

4. Each container of potato salad feeds four people. How many people would two containers feed?

5. 2 × 6

Down

6. 3 × 2

7. 2 × 2

8. Joey has five people in his family. Each person in his family was given four water balloons. How many water balloons did they have?

9. 3 × 3

10. 4 × 4

11. Each person in Joey's family ate two hot dogs. How many hot dogs did Joey's family of five people eat?

Solve the multiplication problems.

At the family picnic, what did one potato chip say to the other?

$5 \times 8 =$ _____ **T**

$2 \times 7 =$ _____ **P**

$4 \times 4 =$ _____ **K**

$6 \times 3 =$ _____ **W**

$7 \times 7 =$ _____ **A**

$8 \times 8 =$ _____ **N**

$4 \times 3 =$ _____ **D**

$7 \times 6 =$ _____ **I**

$8 \times 7 =$ _____ **O**

$3 \times 7 =$ _____ **E**

Write the letters that go with your answers in the blanks below. Write each letter above that answer's number.

___	___	___	___		___	___
18	49	64	40		40	56

___	___	___	___		___	___	___	___?
40	49	16	21		49	12	42	14

Follow the directions in the sunburst.

1 × 4

40 ÷ 10

2 × 2

4 × 6

32 ÷ 8

1. Find two multiplication facts that have an answer of 36. Put a circle around each of them.

8 × 3

40 ÷ 5

2. Find five multiplication facts that have an answer of 24. Put a rectangle around each of them.

3. Find three multiplication or division facts that have an answer of 8. Put a triangle around each of them.

1 × 24

24 ÷ 3

4. Find four multiplication and division facts that have an answer of 4. Draw an X over each of them.

2 × 4

2 × 12

9 × 4

6 × 6

3 × 8

Multiplying through 10

> **Use the clues and multiply!**

Figure out how many people attended each picnic.

At the Jasper family picnic, eight people sat at each of the seven tables. How many people were at the picnic? _____

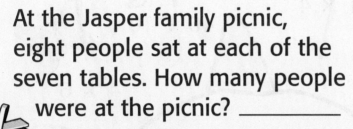

The entire Westley family drove to the picnic in nine cars. Each car carried four people. How many people were at the picnic? _____

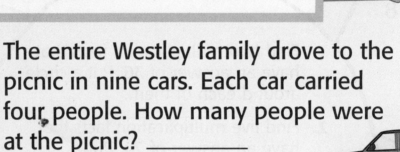

The Chan family's soccer game had six teams with six people on each team. How many people played soccer? _____

At the Hernandez family picnic, eight families attended. Each family brought three people. How many people were at the picnic? _____

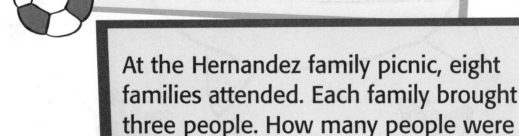

Multiplying through 11

Multiply the two numbers next to the picnic items. Draw a line from each item to the answer on the picnic blanket.

8 × 12 = ____

1 × 11 = ____

2 × 11 = ____

10 × 12 = ____

2 × 12 = ____

9 × 11 = ____

0 × 12 = ____

5 × 11 = ____

96

120

55

11

22

0

24

99

Multiplying

Multiply the numbers below to find the product. Then find the product on the next page and color its block. Coloring the correct products will get you to the sandwich!

When you multiply numbers, the answer is called the product.

1. 9 × 4
2. 6 × 5
3. 3 × 7
4. 8 × 4
5. 3 × 5
6. 1 × 10
7. 9 × 8
8. 7 × 6
9. 4 × 6
10. 9 × 3

11. 3 × 8
12. 4 × 7
13. 5 × 5
14. 6 × 9
15. 10 × 7
16. 8 × 2
17. 7 × 7
18. 3 × 4
19. 2 × 9
20. 6 × 8

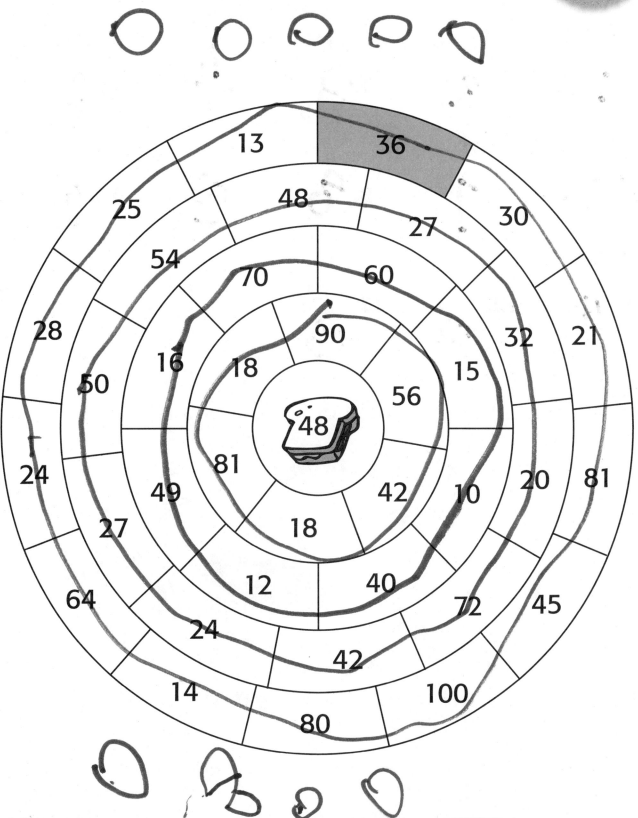

Multiplying 2-Digit Numbers

Multiply the following numbers.

1. 23
× 3
———
69

2. 42
× 2

3. 11
× 8

4. 12
× 4

5. 22
× 3

6. 17
× 1

7. 11
× 3

8. 34
× 2

9. 10
× 6

10. 12
× 3

11. 43
× 1

12. 11
× 5

13. 21
× 3

Now connect the dots in the order of your answers.

Modeling Multiplication

Let's model 14 × 3.

Draw fourteen jelly beans.

> It's sometimes easier to see a model of a problem. **Modeling** means creating a drawing or model of a problem to help you think it through!

Draw fourteen more jelly beans.

And draw fourteen more jelly beans.

Color each set of ten jelly beans a different color.

The number of colors you used is the tens digit of your answer. _____

The number of jelly beans left is the ones digit of your answer. _____

14 × 3 = _____ _____

Multiplying 2-Digit Numbers

In the picture on the next page, color the area that has the answer to each of these problems brown:

10 × 2	10 × 5	10 × 9	11 × 5	11 × 9	12 × 4

12 × 8	13 × 3	13 × 7	12 × 5	16 × 2

Color the area that has the answer to each
of these problems green:

10 × 1	11 × 2	11 × 6	12 × 3	12 × 9	13 × 4	13 × 8	14 × 2	14 × 4

Color the area that has the answer to each
of these problems red:

10 × 3	10 × 7	11 × 3	11 × 7	12 × 2

12 × 6	13 × 1	13 × 5

> Look carefully at the picture. Answers can sometimes be in more than one spot!

13 × 9	14 × 3

Multiplying 2-Digit Numbers

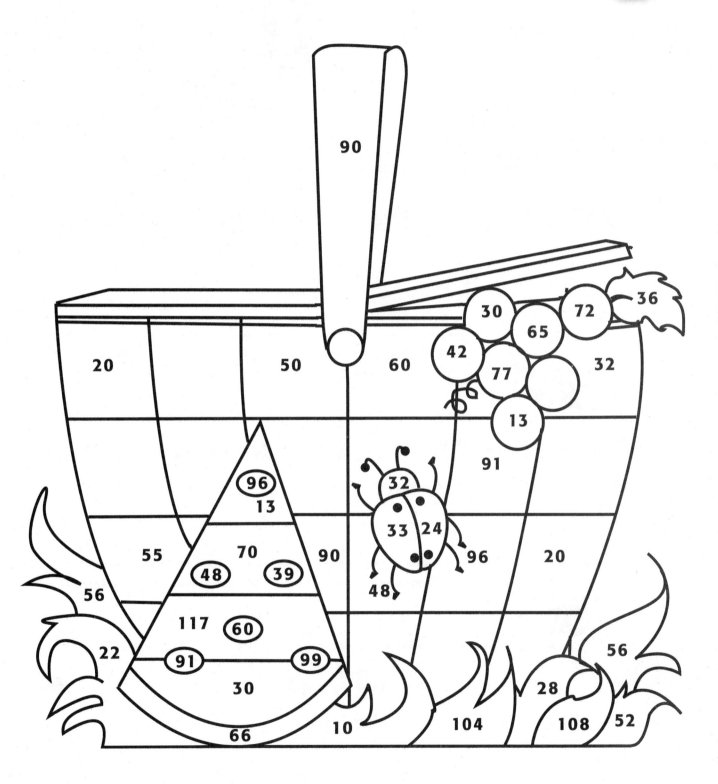

It helps to cross out the items as you subtract from the total number.

Write a subtraction problem to go with each division problem.

8 ÷ 4

8 − ___ − ___ = 0

How many times did you subtract 4? ____

So, 8 ÷ 4 = ____.

10 ÷ 2

10 − ___ − ___ − ___ − ___ − ___ = 0

How many times did you subtract 2? ____

So, 10 ÷ 2 = ____.

12 ÷ 3

12 − ___ − ___ − ___ − ___ = 0

How many times did you subtract 3? ____

So, 12 ÷ 3 = ____.

Dividing into Groups

Figure out how many people will be on each flying disk team. Divide the number of people at each picnic by the number of flying disk teams needed.

1.

$$\frac{15 \text{ people}}{3 \text{ teams}} = \underline{\ 5\ }$$

2.

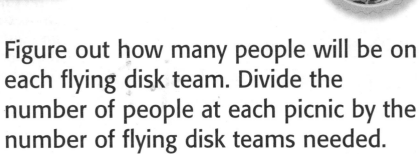

$$\frac{5 \text{ people}}{5 \text{ teams}} = \underline{\quad}$$

3.

$$\frac{8 \text{ people}}{2 \text{ teams}} = \underline{\quad}$$

4.

$$\frac{9 \text{ people}}{3 \text{ teams}} = \underline{\quad}$$

5.

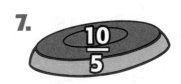

$$\frac{7 \text{ people}}{1 \text{ team}} = \underline{\quad}$$

6.

$$\frac{12 \text{ people}}{2 \text{ teams}} = \underline{\quad}$$

7.

$$\frac{10 \text{ people}}{5 \text{ teams}} = \underline{\quad}$$

8.

$$\frac{18 \text{ people}}{2 \text{ teams}} = \underline{\quad}$$

Identifying Fact Families

Write the number that completes each fact family.

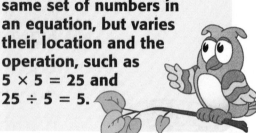

A fact family uses the same set of numbers in an equation, but varies their location and the operation, such as $5 \times 5 = 25$ and $25 \div 5 = 5$.

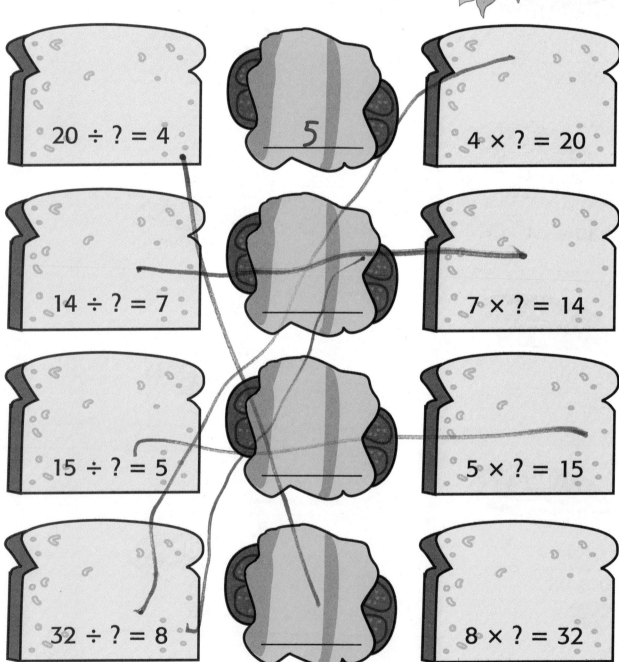

$20 \div ? = 4$

5

$4 \times ? = 20$

$14 \div ? = 7$

_____

$7 \times ? = 14$

$15 \div ? = 5$

_____

$5 \times ? = 15$

$32 \div ? = 8$

_____

$8 \times ? = 32$

Identifying Fact Families

Read each set of questions, and figure out which numbers are in each fact family.

Example: When you multiply us you get 32, and when you divide us you get 2. What numbers are we? __8__ and __4__

When you multiply us you get 12, and when you divide us you get 3. What numbers are we? _____ and _____

When you multiply us you get 7, and when you divide us you get 7. What numbers are we? _____ and _____

When you multiply us you get 27, and when you divide us you get 3. What numbers are we? _____ and _____

Dividing through 4

Read these word problems, and figure out how many of each item is needed.

Ryan has thirty-two orange slices. How many slices should he give four kids so that they each get the same amount? ___2___

The Otter Twins baked nine cookies to share with Ryan. How many cookies does each of them get? ___3___

Ryan needs to select two teams from a total of eighteen kids. How many kids should be on each team? ___

There are sixteen kites. How many kites does each of four kids get? ___5___

Solve these division problems.

1. 49 ÷ 7 = _____   6. 25 ÷ 5 = _____

2. 36 ÷ 4 = _____   7. 16 ÷ 4 = _____

3. 40 ÷ 5 = _____   8. 50 ÷ 5 = _____

4. 18 ÷ 3 = _____   9. 12 ÷ 6 = _____

5. 21 ÷ 7 = _____   10. 20 ÷ 10 = _____

Color the spaces in which the answers are found.

Riddle: What kind of fish goes best with a peanut butter sandwich?

To solve this riddle, first solve these division problems.

1. $27 \div 9 =$ _____ F

2. $35 \div 5 =$ _____ L   6. $100 \div 10 =$ _____ J

3. $72 \div 8 =$ _____ Y   7. $14 \div 7 =$ _____ H

4. $18 \div 3 =$ _____ A   8. $32 \div 4 =$ _____ S

5. $36 \div 9 =$ _____ E   9. $45 \div 9 =$ _____ I

Now write the letters that go with your answers in the blanks above the problems' numbers.

_____ _____ _____ _____ _____ _____
 6   10   4   7   7   9

_____ _____ _____ _____
 3   5   8   2

Identifying Fact Families

Draw a line to connect each fact family in the left column with its matching family in the right column.

$3 \times 5 = 15$

$64 \div 8 = 8$

$8 \times 4 = 32$

$32 \div 8 = 4$

$6 \times 7 = 42$

$54 \div 9 = 6$

$6 \times 9 = 54$

$15 \div 3 = 5$

$8 \times 8 = 64$

$42 \div 7 = 6$

Estimating Multiplication

Estimate the answer to each multiplication problem.

If eighteen people come to the picnic and each person eats about two hot dogs, how many hot dogs should we buy? _____

If twenty-nine people come to the picnic and each person drinks two cans of soda, how many cans should we buy?

_____

If eight people come to the picnic and each person gets about four water balloons, how many balloons should we fill with water?

_____

If eleven people come to the picnic and each person eats about three cookies, how many cookies should we bake?_____

Rounding Numbers

Round each double-digit below to find a compatible number. Then solve each multiplication problem using the compatible number. The first one is done for you.

For each answer less than 100, color the square green.

Compatible numbers are numbers that you use to make it easy to think through math problems.

What a colorful tablecloth for a picnic

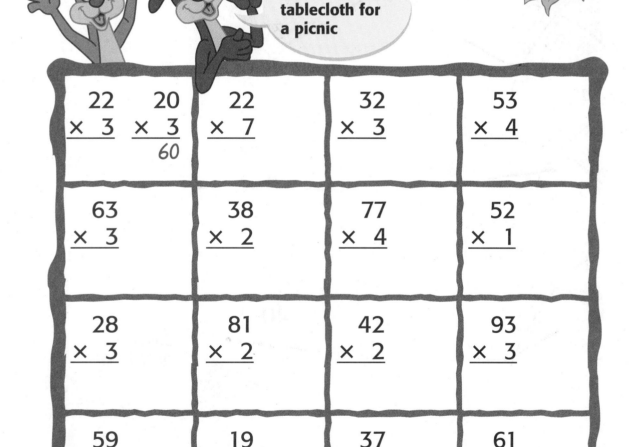

22 20 × 3 × 3 60	22 × 7	32 × 3	53 × 4
63 × 3	38 × 2	77 × 4	52 × 1
28 × 3	81 × 2	42 × 2	93 × 3
59 × 4	19 × 3	37 × 4	61 × 1

Estimating Division

Estimate the answers in the division problems below.
Then draw a line from each problem to its correct answer.

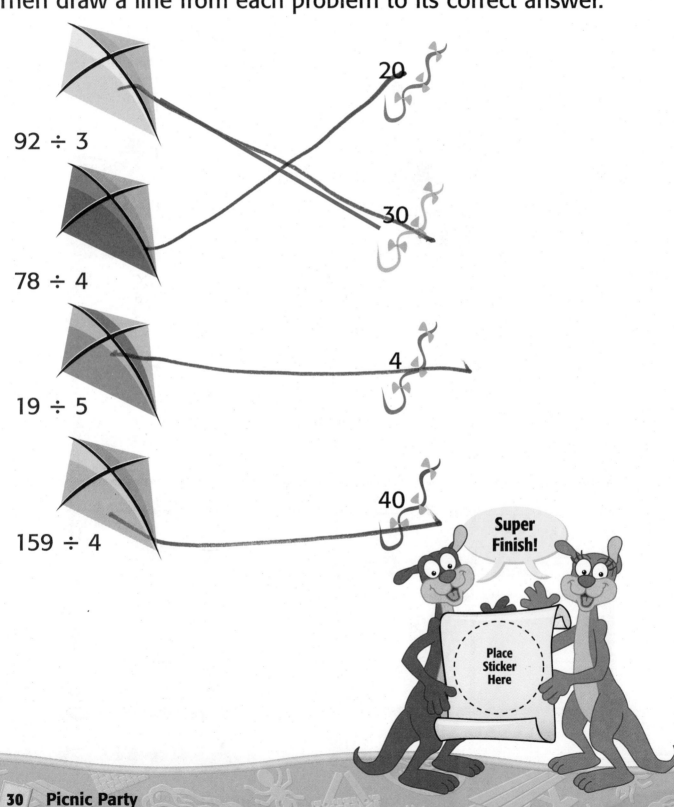

92 ÷ 3

78 ÷ 4

19 ÷ 5

159 ÷ 4

20

30

4

40

Super Finish!

Place Sticker Here

Answer Key

Page 2: Logic Feature

Ina–drinks; Al–hot dogs; Ken–cookies

Page 3: Mental Math Feature

1, 2, 3, 4, 5, 6; 2, 4, 6, 8, 10, 12;
3, 6, 9, 12, 15, 18; 4, 8, 12, 16, 20, 24;
5, 10, 15, 20, 25, 30; 6, 12, 18, 24, 30, 36;
7, 14, 21, 28, 35, 42; 8, 16, 24, 32, 40, 48;
9, 18, 27, 36, 45, 54

Page 4: Adding Repeated Numbers

$2 + 2 + 2 = 2 \times 3 = 6$;
$1 + 1 + 1 + 1 + 1 = 1 \times 5 = 5$;
$4 + 4 = 4 \times 2 = 8$

Page 5: Relating Addition

$\times 4$, $6 \times$

Page 6: Multiplying through 2

2. 5; 5 hamburgers
3. 4; 4 slices of watermelon
4. 12; 12 sandwiches
5. 2; 2 ice cream cones

Page 7: Multiplying through 4

32 packages of hamburgers, 20 bags of chips, 12 dozen cookies, 28 bottles of fruit drink

Page 8: Problem-Solving Feature

Step 1: 16
Step 2: 16, 10, 6
Step 3: 6, 2; 3

Page 9: Multiplying through 6

Across: 2. thirty; 3. fifteen;
4. eight; 5. twelve; Down: 6. six;
7. four; 8. twenty; 9. nine;
10. sixteen; 11. ten

Page 10: Multiplying through 8

T = 40; P = 14; K = 16; W = 18; A = 49;
N = 64; D = 12; I = 42; O = 56; E = 21;
Want to take a dip?

Page 11: Visual Feature

1. 6×6 and 9×4.
2. 4×6, 8×3, 1×24, 2×12 and 3×8.
3. 2×4, $24 \div 3$, and $40 \div 5$.
4. $32 \div 8$, 2×2, 1×4, and $40 \div 10$.

Page 12: Multiplying through 10

56; 36; 36; 24

Page 13: Multiplying through 11

96; 11; 22; 120; 24; 99; 0; 55

Page 14: Multiplying

1. 36	11. 24
2. 30	12. 28
3. 21	13. 25
4. 32	14. 54
5. 15	15. 70
6. 10	16. 16
7. 72	17. 49
8. 42	18. 12
9. 24	19. 18
10. 27	20. 48

Page 16: Multiplying 2-Digit Numbers

84, 88, 48, 66, 17, 33, 68, 60, 36, 43, 55, 63; connecting the dots reveals a radio.

Page 17: Modeling Multiplication

4 sets of 10; 2 ones; $14 \times 3 = 42$

Answer Key

Page 18, 19: Multiplying 2-Digit Numbers

Brown: 20, 50, 90, 55, 99, 48, 96, 39, 91, 60, 32; Green: 10, 22, 66, 36, 108, 52, 104, 28, 56; Red: 30, 70, 33, 77, 24, 72, 13, 65, 117, 42. The picture is a picnic basket with grapes, a slice of watermelon, and a ladybug. The picnic basket is sitting in the grass.

Page 20: Dividing with Repeated Subtraction

$8 - 4 - 4$; 2, $8 ÷ 4 = 2$; $10 - 2 - 2 - 2 - 2 - 2$; 5, $10 ÷ 2 = 5$;
$12 - 3 - 3 - 3 - 3$; 4, $12 ÷ 3 = 4$

Page 21: Dividing into Groups

2. 1 person per team
3. 4 people per team
4. 3 people per team
5. 7 people per team
6. 6 people per team
7. 2 people per team
8. 9 people per team

Page 22: Identifying Fact Families

2; 3; 4

Page 23: Identifying Fact Families

6 and 2; 7 and 1; 9 and 3

Page 24: Dividing through 4

8 slices; 3 cookies; 9 kids; 4 kites

Page 25: Dividing through 7

7; 9; 8; 6; 3; 5; 4; 10; 2; 2; the picture will show a picnic scene.

Page 26: Dividing through 10

F = 3; L = 7; Y = 9; A = 6; E = 4; J = 10; H = 2; S = 8; I = 5; a jellyfish

Page 27: Identifying Fact Families

$8 × 4 = 32$ and $32 ÷ 8 = 4$;
$6 × 7 = 42$ and $42 ÷ 7 = 6$;
$6 × 9 = 54$ and $54 ÷ 9 = 6$;
$8 × 8 = 64$ and $64 ÷ 8 = 8$

Page 28: Estimating Multiplication

40 hot dogs; 60 cans of soda; 30 water balloons; 30 cookies

Page 29: Rounding Numbers

140; 90, colored green; 200; 180; 80, colored green; 320; 50, colored green; 90, colored green; 160; 80, colored green; 270; 240; 60, colored green; 160; 60, colored green

Page 30: Estimating Division

$78 ÷ 4$ is about 20; $19 ÷ 5$ is about 4; $159 ÷ 4$ is about 40.